Goodnight Dad
Written by Tommy Watkins

To my dad Paul, and all the years watching Chicago Sports with you. I will always carry these memories for the rest of my life.

"Wake up! The big game is on!" said
Dad.

I ran downstairs, made my favorite cereal, and watched the game.

3D
CRCAL
3D
CURCAE

The game ended with our team winning by a field goal. Our night was about to beginning going to the hockey game!

We arrive at the arena, find our seats, and go to the concession stand to orde Italian Beef sandwiches.

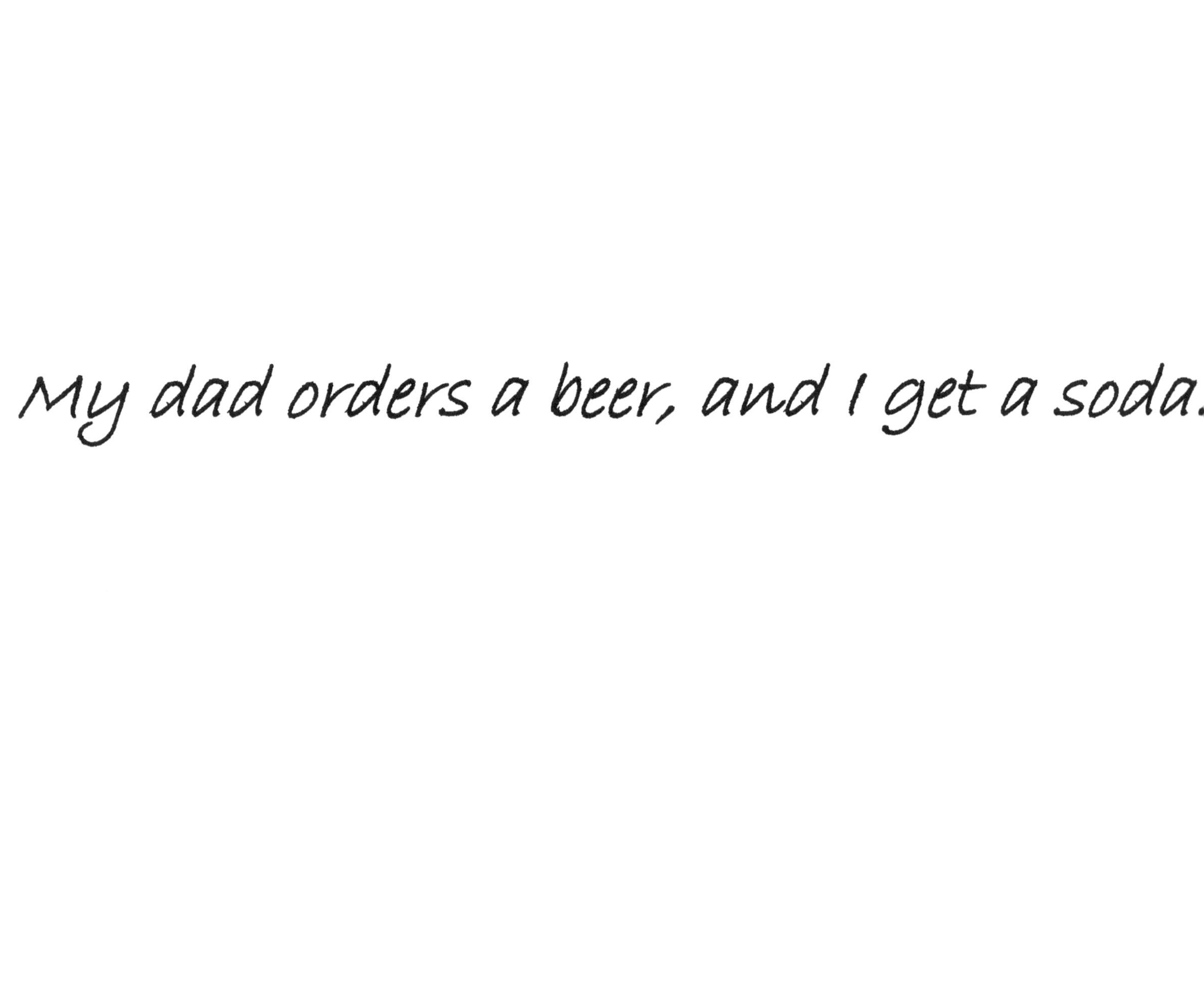
My dad orders a beer, and I get a soda.

Oéxin

We watch the hockey game excited wit.
the outcome.

Our favorite team wins in the final seconds of the game.

We drive home listening to the local radio station recapping the win.

As I get home, my dad and I go to bed after a fantastic day.

"Goodnight Dad." I said.

The End

9 798330 237678